Lean Into Your Light

Unleash the divine spirit within and create your life with intention

MaryEllen Whitton

little pink press

Lean Into Your Light

Copyright © 2024 MaryEllen Whitton

All rights reserved. No part of this book may be reproduced or retransmitted in any form or by any means without the written permission of the publisher.

Cover design: Keryl Pesce

Published by Little Pink Press, Beacon, NY

ISBN-13: 979-8-9870085-7-7

Dedication

For Caitlyn Jayne

Contents

Section 1 – The Back Story and Big Picture

Introduction	1
Your Successful Life	15
Energy and Vibration	25

Section 2 – Tips, Tricks, and Tools

Advocate for Your Success	37
The Power of Imagination	39
Breathe	41
Shifting to Desire and Intention	43
The Top Three	49
No Regrets	53
Emotions and Feelings	57
Believe	65
Cultivate a Gratitude Practice	69
Music	73
Colors	75

Patience and Repetition	77
Habits	79
Meditation	85
Passwords	89
Fitness and Food	91
Releasing Resistance	95
Make Peace with Your Past	97
Do Something!	101
Reciprocity	105

Section 3 — Golden Words

The "I Am" Process	111
Quality of Life	119
Your Physical Body	125
Relationships	127
Financial	129
Spiritual	131
My Happy List	134
My Gratitude List	135
My Food Journal	136
Old Beliefs and Resistances I Am Releasing	139

Do Something	140
Not-To-Do List	141
How My Life Will Look	142
About the Author	143

Acknowledgments

First, this book wouldn't exist without my daughter, so thank you, Caitlyn, for this gift born out of a place of darkness.

Second, to my son Alex and my friends who gave of their time and love to read and share their honest thoughts, ideas, and suggestions: Dr. Kimberley McGrath-Salamone, Dawn Robles, Jenny Sharon, Mali Kigasari, Beverly Ruggiero, Delaina Petraglia, Sue Krebs (author of *Ego-Spirit Thinking*) and my new friend and publisher, Keryl Pesce.

*Watch your thoughts,
for they become words.*

*Watch your words,
for they become actions.*

*Watch your actions,
for they become habits.*

*Watch your habits,
for they become character.*

*Watch your character,
for it becomes your destiny.*

~ Lao Tzu

Section 1

The Back Story and Big Picture

Introduction

The book you hold in your hands can create radical change in your life. How do I know? First-hand experience. Before we get into the content, I want to offer full disclosure here. If it's a resume you're interested in, I'm not your girl. I am neither a psychologist nor a metaphysician. Who I am is a mom who deeply loves her daughter. You see, several years ago, my beautiful and brilliant daughter was struggling as a young adult. Her self-esteem and self-worth were almost non-existent.

While the reality was, and is, that she is intelligent and capable, she had come to believe a lie that she was anything but. Who fed her these lies? She did. With her silent yet screaming self-talk as well as the words she openly voiced. She went through a long period during which whenever she called or texted me, she always started with some variation of: "I am frustrated, I am stressed, or I am disappointed."

This type of communication went on for many months. I explained to my daughter that when she thinks, says, and feels strongly, "I am frustrated," "I am stressed," or "I am disappointed," she is inviting more frustration, stress, and disappointment into her life.

We all sometimes feel this way, and it is a normal part of life. However, since she constantly focused on and repeated these statements, she was unknowingly matching her vibrational energy with frustration, stress, and disappointment. She was attracting more of the same into her life.

In Hebrew, Abracadabra essentially translates to "I create as I speak." Instinctively, I knew she needed new words, new thought patterns, and the creation of a new identity with the literal magic of the words she chose. I began texting her positive "I AM" statements. One day, I asked if she was reading the "I AM" statements I had texted her. She said she hadn't. Knowing how stubborn she can be, I wasn't surprised. So, I decided to take a different route. Since I know how much she loves books, I bought a blank, spiral-bound artist's sketchbook. I hand-wrote her a book of positive "I AM" statements using a gold Sharpie.

One afternoon, her "I AM" book was on my kitchen counter, and her friend who was visiting, picked it up. She said that she loved it and asked if she could have one. I said yes, but not that one. I told her that I would make one just for her. The next day, I returned to the store and purchased another sketchbook to hand-write a copy for my daughter's friend. That was my "Aha" moment, and I thought, hmmm, if she likes this, how many more people will like this material? So, I asked myself, how about turning my notes into a book for the benefit of others?

This book was born out of my desire to help my daughter. What started as positive "I AM" statements to help lift her mood took on a life of its own in the most wonderful ways, including pulling me out of a dark place when I needed it most. A few simple words crafted to help her, profoundly changed my life. My intention is they will change yours as well. I had no idea a few hand-written notes would lead me down a path of discovery of the power we all hold within ourselves to alter our perspectives, thoughts, and lives.

The best place to start this journey is with awareness, which is simply your perception or knowledge of something. This book will assist you in developing a keen awareness of what you think, feel, and truly believe, which is the first step in the transformation process. You might also hear awareness referred to as consciousness or mindfulness; it's essentially the same thing. Change begins when you become aware, conscious, or mindful of something.

As you begin the process of self-awareness, you need to understand that your thoughts, feelings, and core beliefs carry tremendous power...the capability to direct your life and to influence how you feel and what you experience. And this, my friend, is precisely what it means to *Lean Into Your Light*. You are light. You are love. You are powerful. It's time to lean into all of that and actively shape your life experience. In the following pages, you will learn why it works and how easy it is.

It's your light that lights the world.

~Rumi

As you read on and integrate what you learn, you will become aware of thoughts and beliefs you hold that are not true and do not serve you. There are simple shifts to apply to your inner and outer dialogue and help you break through these negative thinking habits and self-limiting beliefs that create barriers to your desires, aspirations, and joy. Replacing negative thinking habits (and behaviors), which don't feel good and are generally a waste of your time and energy, with better-feeling thoughts (and behaviors) opens new possibilities. Ultimately, this brings about transformation; as I mentioned, this is my intention for you.

Through awareness, you will awaken and transform any core beliefs that were negative and false into ones that serve and support your highest ideals. This will help you create and develop your true, authentic self.

Of the approximately eight billion people on the planet, there is only one YOU! As the 19th-Century poet and playwright Oscar Wilde suggested, "Be yourself; everyone else is already taken."

You have unique and valuable gifts, talents, and purposes that your heart and soul need to express. Use this book as inspiration to live out your dreams, achieve your goals, and live your true calling. You will create foundational happiness, contentment, and fulfillment by cultivating, nurturing, and sharing your gifts and talents. You will thrive by living your life's purpose, which will enrich and add value to the lives of others, creating a ripple effect on those around you. What a pleasure it will be to watch them start thriving, too!

I personally define happiness as "A state of being, deep inside, feeling content, confident, and peaceful." It does not mean life is rainbows and butterflies 24/7. You will have good days, great days, and some really bad days. One day you can feel blissful and then receive news that will turn your world upside down. So, if you start now, you will create an inner foundation to anchor you through the sometimes-wild waves of life.

For me, a solid foundation for a happy life is living by my core values:

- A healthy body, mind, and spirit
- Quality relationships with family/friends/partner/social/career/etc.
- Work/volunteering I enjoy
- Having enough money for my needs and desires plus extra to give away
- Being of value, in some way, every day, to all beings I come in contact with
- Having integrity by expressing my truth (kindly as appropriate) in my words and actions

As I started learning, understanding, and integrating everything you will learn in this book, I decided to make a happy life for myself. For me, it began with consciously surrounding myself with people, objects (like art), and experiences I like, enjoy, and that make me feel good.

For example, I went through my closet, weeded out any attire I didn't feel good wearing and gave it away. Some went to Goodwill, and some went to a local nonprofit that supports homeless people. I even got rid of photos I didn't feel good about when I looked at them. As best as possible, I reduced or eliminated spending time with people I didn't feel good around and going to places I didn't enjoy.

The examples above support my decision to be happier. Making a decision, whether big or small, means cutting off all other possibilities and taking the plunge! What decisions will you make to support your happiness?

I hope this book will be an instrument to bring you and others happiness as well. What began as a notebook to help my daughter blossomed into changing myself and consciously creating my own peace of mind.

It is one of the most beautiful compensations of this life that no man can sincerely try to help another without helping himself.

~Ralph Waldo Emerson

Commit yourself to creating your own life with whatever makes you happy. This doesn't mean you will be grinning from ear to ear every day, but it does mean that you will create an internal stability to weather the storms of life. Right now is the best moment to begin your journey.

It is simply a choice you make. You can devise a hundred excuses for why you can't be happy, joyous, or achieve your goals. Well, guess what? It's just as easy to come up with a hundred reasons why you CAN. An excellent place to start is by celebrating the moments in your day that work out in your favor. I recently learned of a term called a "glimmer" coined by psychotherapist Deb Dana. She defines it as "small moments when our biology is in a place of connection or regulation, which cues our nervous system to feel safe or calm." Pay attention to these glimmers during your day. Pause, enjoy, and appreciate them for as long as you can!

What an amazing world we would have if every one of us were living our authentic selves and living a life that brings us delight as well as using our gifts in service of others. This world is possible, and it starts with you and me together in the pages ahead.

I began to wonder what it means to be authentic. I looked up definitions online and didn't find one that felt like a great fit for this book. Then, shortly before publishing, I was out downtown and spotted this sign outside a shop:

authentic

aw-then-tik
being exactly who you are without any qualification
or apology; true to your own personality, spirit
and character; to be wholly yourself

It was perfect! I was so excited. I took a picture of it and now here it is, making me feel the book is complete. The ultimate freedom in life, I believe, is to be your authentic self.

It has taken me a lifetime to learn everything in this book. Especially the knowledge that I gained during a painful period, which

I refer to as my "dark night of the soul," as the saying goes. Most everyone will experience at least one of these in their lifetime, if not more, when we lose touch with our spark, the divine spirit presence within us.

In my mid-forties, I experienced a series of losses and deaths of people close to me. I had to close my beloved business during the recession in 2009; I had been living my purpose of owning and running a yoga studio and was incredibly happy. After I closed my studio, Zenergy Yoga, I went to seven funerals within about a year's time. The youngest was only 10 years old, and one was a teenage suicide.

The last two were the hardest ones until about a year later, when I experienced the sudden death of my best friend, Roxane. It rocked my world and ripped my heart into a million pieces. I was a mess. The waves of grief would strike me at any time, waking me up in the middle of the night, in the grocery store, at the gas station, and at work. I never knew when or for how long these episodes would occur. I often had to retreat to my car or hide in a restroom. What I eventually learned was to surrender to the grief and let it just be.

Over time, I began feeling seriously depressed, as if my life was meaningless and I had no purpose. I closed myself off, as much as possible, from my friends and family. It got to the point that I didn't believe in myself anymore, lost my self-confidence, and often had suicidal thoughts.

But the truth is that I didn't want to die; I wanted to feel better.

Looking back, it was like I was in a cocoon, shielding my true self from the world…maybe even from myself. After about five years, I was ready to re-emerge as a more gracious, accepting, and gentler version of myself. It allowed me to go deep within myself and eventually give birth to this book.

There is an emerging field of psychology called "Post-Traumatic Growth." It suggests that many people can use their pain, hardships, and traumas and turn them into something good. They found that trauma can produce substantial creative and intellectual development, and that life's hardships can help people grow in interpersonal relationships, contentment, gratitude, personal strength, and resourcefulness. I hadn't a clue this was possible during my most difficult moments, but now, looking back, it makes complete sense to me.

During that period, when I was able to get myself to a calm state of mind, I noticed a small voice inside me saying, "It's not over. You'll get beyond this." What started as a flicker of hope turned into trust and, eventually, faith. I knew in my heart and soul that I would get beyond that stage of my life and not just survive but thrive. Now, I understand that period in my life served a higher purpose: to mold me into a better version of myself, and to use my experiences to serve others.

So, I began reminding myself of the things I had done well and am proud of. I began hanging them up in my mind's hallway. In my journal, I wrote lists of things that made me feel happy. Then I decided to write them on poster boards, which I taped to the walls in my house, to see them easily. Thankfully, I lived alone at the time. It probably would look a little nutty to someone else, but I didn't care; it worked for me!

As I started feeling a little better, I wondered, "What have I learned from what I've gone through?" and "How can I move forward?" It propelled me into a quest of discovery.

I felt inspired to research and study how to design and create happiness in my future life. I took an online course that showed up in my inbox one day and felt like a great fit. It focused on creating all aspects of my life into 12 significant categories. This tied together the countless books I'd read into one document that I created, my own Lifebook. It had, and still has, a profound impact on my life. It brought me to this point and continues to be a blueprint for my life. I read it quarterly and annually update for the next year ahead.

From all the knowledge I accumulated, what I learned can be summed up in a simple two-part equation:

Vibration = Attraction

1. Your thoughts, feelings, and beliefs vibrate and emit a frequency, The Law of Vibration.

2. The frequency you are vibrating at determines what is attracted to you, The Law of Attraction.

That's it!

It is truly that simple, yet not always easy, mainly because we get in our own way with resistance and beliefs that do not align with our true desires and intentions (more on this later).

Your thoughts, feelings, and beliefs create the vibration that allows the magnetic Law of Attraction to bring your desires to you. Keep bringing yourself back to these two core concepts.

As you read on, you will realize what a powerful creator you are, and that *you* are in charge of the trajectory of your life. Keep practicing and integrating what you learn in this book into your daily life.

You will transform yourself by learning, applying, and assimilating these simple concepts into your daily life. You will manifest your best life by consciously and intentionally creating whatever you desire to be, do, or have! And the ripple effect will expand and positively influence those around you. In the rest of this book, I provide background, explanations, and examples for you to practice.

I also define many common, everyday words we use regularly. Knowing the true meaning behind these words will help you refine your thoughts and speech to reflect most accurately what you intend to communicate and attract. You will notice quite a few of these words are in the ancient language of Sanskrit. As a yoga student and teacher for over 25 years, I have been learning and exploring this beautiful, expressive language.

It is said each letter of the Sanskrit alphabet has a corresponding sound vibration in both the subtle energy channels of our bodies and in the cosmos. These are known as Matrikas or Mother Wheels. This is the force that can cause a spark, a movement that changes your life. Matrika reveals itself when awareness starts and you walk toward a new path. This is an example of how powerful language is.

Back in the 1970's, Richard Bandler and John Grinder founded a field of study called Neurolinguistic Programming (NLP). This discipline proves there is a correlation between the brain, body, language, behaviors, senses, gut instinct, and intuition. I couldn't agree more.

Something drew you to this book, so read on and enjoy your quest for discovery, learning, and growth. And, remember to enjoy the ride; the joy is in our journey, not the destination. You don't ski down a mountain just to get to the bottom!

And, this is not a book to read once and put on the shelf. Think of it as more of a companion. Keep it nearby at home and put it in your bag when you leave the house. Take it out on breaks at work or while waiting for an appointment. After you read it for the first time, put it on your calendar to read it again in a month, and whenever you feel the nudge, open it to any random page. It will deliver the message you most need at that moment.

I see how far I have come in practicing and integrating this knowledge in my own life. I see the evidence daily; I am happier, and my intentions continue to become reality, including writing and publishing this book. And now, dear reader, you being here with me brings my dream to life by sharing what I've learned with you so that you may live a little better, or a whole lot better, from here on out.

Feel free to get a highlighter, a pen, a Sharpie, whatever works for you, and make this learning experience uniquely yours. Take notes, draw, and doodle everywhere.

This book touches on many aspects of self-development, and I encourage you to continue reading and educating yourself. Please visit my website, www.leanintoyourlightbook.com for a deeper dive.

Your Successful Life

The whole secret of a successful life is to find out what is one's destiny and then do it.

~Henry Ford

How do you define your successful life? Not what your parents, teachers, friends, partner, or children might think. You. Beautiful, brilliant, you.

When we were babies and young children, we had no issues with being or expressing ourselves. We trusted ourselves to know what we wanted and let our desires be known. As we grew up, however, we somehow learned to filter our true aspirations through concern with others' opinions. Although many people close to us are well-meaning, what we truly want for ourselves often gets clouded by their influence. Now it's time to let the clouds lift and get clear on what you want to become and create for yourself, no matter where you are in your life's journey.

We talk a lot about success, but what does that truly mean? I found a great definition of success by the legendary author Earl Nightingale, known for his writings on the subjects of character development, motivation, and meaningful existence:

> *Success is really nothing more than the progressive realization of a working ideal. This means that any person who knows what they are doing and where they are going is a success. Any person with a goal towards which they are working is a successful person.*

What does success mean to you? It means different things to different people. It's not just about having a lot of money or fame. There are plenty of wealthy and famous people who seem unhappy. And many people are poor, by our standards, yet appear genuinely happy and content.

Doing things that make me happy, with people I care about, and appreciating all I have is how I define success.

Create your own definition of success:

_____

_____

_____

Lean Into Your Light

I was fascinated by South America and traveled there when I was in my twenties. I started in Bolivia, then Peru, backpacking the Inca Trail to Machu Picchu, and finished in Ecuador.

While backpacking through the Andes countryside, I came across families living in stone huts, in the middle of nowhere. They came out of their homes to greet me, smiling and enthusiastic to have a visitor and chatted with me in my limited Spanish.

What struck me the most and has stayed with me all these years later is how it felt to me that these people were truly happy! By our standards, they had nothing. These folks didn't have indoor plumbing, electricity, or a car. They had few material possessions and very little money.

I believe that they had something far greater than those things. They had love and appreciation for everything they did have. They seemed to appreciate being alive and being together with their families. I could feel they vibrated at the highest levels of the emotional scale. For a visual chart of the vibrational scale, please go to my Facebook page, Lean Into Your Light.

Need some guidance and inspiration for discovering and defining your purpose? I recently read *The Path Made Clear: Discovering Your Life's Direction and Purpose* by Oprah Winfrey. In it, she states, "There is no greater gift you can give or receive than to honor your calling. It's why you were born. And how you become most truly alive."

You are a vessel, stewarding and carrying unique gifts and

talents. Bring them forth into the world. Your life is an expression of your spirit.

Some people know their purpose at a young age. Others discover or rediscover it later in life. Many of us, myself included, have different passions and purposes throughout our lives. Whatever the case, enjoy the adventure once you know what it is.

The eloquent writer Dawna Markova says: "What are your gifts and talents? Most of us reasonably articulate about our deficits and weaknesses-how many we got wrong on our spelling tests, how many things we have failed to accomplish any given day. We become fluent at explaining our incompetencies but look straight over our gifts and talents and then mutter, "Oh, that old thing?" This leaves us awkward and confused about how to bring forth our assets and resources to the rest of the community. Too many of us believe we don't matter, and that what we do doesn't really make a difference."

The truth is, who you are and what you do DOES matter. Who you are may influence one person or millions. That isn't what is most important, however. What is most important is that you share your unique gifts.

The famous artist Pablo Picasso said, "The meaning of life is to find your gift. The purpose of life is to give it away." In Picasso's case, his art continues to bring joy and appreciation to many people today.

We all have different gifts, talents, and ambitions. Our commonality is that we give it away in service to others. That is our why. As the saying goes, "Once you know your why, you'll find your way." And the famous Mark Twain quote: "The two most important days in your life are the day you were born and the day you find out why."

Discovering and living our why, is a common thread through all of humanity. It is crucial. Many cultures have a name for this.

Here are a few examples:

- The Japanese call it "ikigai" meaning "a reason to get up in the morning."

- In French, it is known as "raison d'etre" which translates to a "reason for being."

- In Sanskrit, it's known as sankalpa, meaning "connection with your highest truth and vow to live your true purpose."

To keep myself focused on my purpose, I created my own Personal Intention Statement. I printed it in purple ink (a meaningful color, more later) and have it framed in my office:

My Life's Intention:

*To continually develop myself as a
teacher and leader while serving others.*

Create your Life's Intention here:

_____

_____

_____

Getting in alignment with your purpose takes time. There is a beautiful word in Sanskrit: Svadhyaya. It's translated as "Be studious; study yourself through introspection. Discover which thoughts, actions, words, and experiences actually make you feel good." This is self-care at its best. Get to really know yourself.

Your purpose, goals, and intentions will change and evolve over your lifetime. For example, my purpose relative to my family is different now than when my children were babies. I also had not considered writing a book, yet the calling, my purpose, was so strong I had to!

And, if you need a nudge in finding your purpose, let the following questions guide you. They all ask the same thing in different ways:

What interests and inspires you? What makes you feel excited and truly alive? What lights you up and what makes you feel whole and complete? What makes your heart sing?

_____

What do you get totally immersed in when time doesn't feel like it exists?

_____

What *must* you accomplish in your life to feel complete?

_____

What are you talented at *and* what do you enjoy doing? (You can be good at something and not enjoy it.)

_____

What contributions do you feel compelled to make to your family, friends, community, or the world?

_____

How would you live your life if you were guaranteed success, as you define it?

_____

These are profound questions. Get quiet and listen for the answers within your heart. Be curious about what comes forth. Just asking these questions creates momentum. In this case, the motion is your thoughts. And all movement has momentum. It's a fundamental law of physics: an object in motion stays in motion, and an object at rest stays at rest.

Get those thought juices flowing! Get yourself in motion! It feels exciting and propels you toward your dreams, desires, and intentions.

Follow your bliss.
~Joseph Campbell

Let your "work" be a form of self-expression, rather than just income for survival. As a matter of fact, don't think of "working." Rather, frame it as, "How can I serve others?" Not sharing your gifts is actually a disservice to others who need what you have to offer. Same goes for anyone denying their true calling and offering it to the rest of us.

What occupies your thoughts? My son, who loves to garden and grow vegetables, told me he thinks about dirt all day at work! He knows his why and is working his day job with the intention of buying land so he can farm. What I think about all day is this book. I know my why, and I am making it happen. It exhilarates me to think about you not just reading this book, but truly creating a miraculous life that brings you fulfillment, contentment, and prosperity.

"At the center of your being you have the answer, you know who you are, and you know what you want," as the sage Lao Tzu discovered.

The wise sage Rumi said, "What you are seeking is seeking you."

In his commencement speech to the 2014 class of the Maharishi International University, comedian Jim Carrey said, "I learned many great lessons from my father, not the least of which was that you can fail at what you don't want so you might as well take a chance on doing what you love." Among many other wise nuggets, he also said, "The effect you have on others is the most valuable currency you have." I highly recommend watching it on YouTube.

Here are a few examples to think about:

> What if Tina Fey or Jimmy Fallon didn't follow their passions to make us laugh?
>
> What if J.K. Rowlings, creator of Harry Potter, was too worried about what other people would think and didn't follow her passion to creatively write? She has captured the imagination and hearts of millions across the world.
>
> How about Tina Turner, the Queen of Rock? What if she didn't believe in herself and never shared her musical gifts with the world?

Pick three of your favorite comedians, artists, musicians, actors, etc. Then, ask yourself, "What if they didn't follow their hearts?" You, me, and the world would have missed out on these great talents, inspirations, and creators:

1. _____

2. _____

3. _____

The truth is the world needs you to follow your heart and your passion(s) too.

Energy and Vibration

Everything is energy, and energy is consciousness and awareness.

~Dr. Joe Dispenza

What am I? What are you? We all are energy and vibration.

Energy cannot be created or destroyed, however it can change its form. It has no boundaries and cannot be contained. You can't store it in a box.

Vibration is the never-ending motion of particles. Every element in the Universe, including every microscopic cell in your body, vibrates and pulses at a particular frequency.

This is known as the Law of Vibration, the first and most powerful Universal Law. It governs the entire Universe. First there is vibration, and then secondly, the magnetic Law of Attraction, which states like attracts like, aligns with the vibration. It's not a force like magnetism, it *IS* magnetism. There is an invisible magnetic beacon inside of you and all around you.

Over 60 years ago, Catherine Ponder wrote these timeless words: "I am an irresistible magnet, with the power to attract unto myself everything that I divinely desire, according to the thoughts, feelings, and mental pictures I constantly entertain and radiate."

Choose your words wisely, whether you are talking to yourself or with others. Refine them to align with higher vibrational and better feeling frequencies.

> *The words we choose to use when we communicate with each other carry vibrations. The word "war" carries a whole different vibration than the word "peace." The words we use show us how we think and how we feel. The careful selection of words helps to elevate our consciousness and resonate in higher frequencies.*
>
> ~Grigoris Deoudis

Say these words and notice how you feel:

    Hate
    Anger
    Revenge

Lean Into Your Light

Now say these words and notice how you feel:

> Love
> Acceptance
> Forgiveness

Whether you or the recipient are aware of it or not, each of these words carries a certain vibration. It goes far beyond the dictionary definition.

If you say a word but are not sincere, the vibration of insincerity will be felt. What comes to mind is when a child (or an adult) does something and is forced to apologize. The words "I'm sorry" come out of their mouth, but the actual message is, "I am not sorry, and now I resent having to say it."

Once the words fall out of your mouth, or you are thinking them, the vibration of your true feeling emanates and energetically pulsates from you.

It's like ringing a bell. Once you ring the bell, you cannot un-ring it. Even if you put your hand on the bell and it stops making sound, its vibrations invisibly pulse through you, around you, and out into the Universe.

You're probably thinking, *Yikes, I said something unkind yesterday, or I had a mean thought.* It's okay. Even though you can't delete them, once you are aware of them, you can shift your attention to something more pleasing and cultivate that vibration. The negative energy will lose momentum.

Here's an example of how to shift energy from negative to positive: re-frame complaints into explanations. It is a simple yet profound game changer. Do you like to listen to anyone complain? Have you ever called a friend to complain? We've all done it and probably will again. Sometimes, we all need to vent and get it off our chests. But in the long run, whether you are dishing it out or listening to someone else, it is ultimately a draining and unproductive experience.

What to do instead? Give up complaining and shift to explaining instead. Complaining keeps you from taking actions, which are solutions, and helps you avoid responsibility. It means you are focusing on the problem and procrastinating on solutions. Explaining, however, opens up an opportunity for feedback and possible solutions. Get into this habit.

On this subject of complaining, do your best to limit your engagement in negative conversations. Avoid watching, reading, and discussing events full of despair, such as we often see on the news. A few minutes here and there are okay. But the longer you watch, read, or talk about them, the easier it will be to slide down the vibrational scale.

Begin to notice any self-destructive, low-vibrational thoughts and weed them from the garden of your mind.

Our minds are hardwired with negative vibrational frequencies, stemming from a survival mechanism I will discuss later. For now, know that you can train yourself to be aware of them and then pivot into neutral or positive thoughts, as appropriate.

Recognize that "negative" emotions and feelings aren't necessarily bad. We have them for a reason. They offer us guidance and feedback about situations. You just don't want to hang onto them too long.

For example, if someone was rude to you and you felt hurt or angry, that's appropriate. However, it was that person's issue, not yours, so you can let it go. If you drag it around all day and tell everyone about it, it's negatively affecting your precious vibration.

Speaking of vibration, thoughts, words, and sounds aren't the only things that vibrate. *Everything* in our physical world vibrates. If you believe your physical body, the food you eat, and the rocks outside are solid, well, think again. Solid is an illusion.

If you put your hand, a banana, or a rock under a high-powered microscope, you will see that none of them are actually solid. Every particle in the Universe vibrates and pulses at a frequency.

Nothing is ever still. As stated in the classic text, *The Kybalion*, "Nothing rests; everything moves; everything vibrates."

Since our Earth home and the entire Universe operate on the Laws of Vibration and Attraction, choose your thoughts and words carefully. Continuously raise your awareness of how you feel. You must learn to cultivate and match the vibrating frequency of your positive intentions. The Universe *always* matches the vibration of the beliefs, feelings, and emotions behind your words.

Practice aligning your thoughts and corresponding emotions. Feel as if your intentions have already been answered, as if it's already done. And, when you are in complete alignment, you come into your full power.

The answer is always "Yes" to whatever you think or talk about, put your attention on, believe, and most of all, feel. The Universe creates through the language of vibration and follows up with attraction to that vibrational offering. Simply stated, you attract what you think about.

It is the basis of our Universe: When it is asked, it is always given. Humans think they are asking with their words or even with their actions — and sometimes you are — but the Universe is not responding to your words or your actions. The Universe is responding to your vibrational calling.

~Abraham/Esther Hicks

For example, if you focus on not wanting something, like more bills or expenses, guess what? You will receive more bills and expenses, exactly what you do not want, because that is your point of attraction. Either re-direct your focus to something neutral or pivot to attracting additional income, as long as it does not cause resistance. When you get to this level, money will often find you.

Recently, I received an unexpected bill. Instead of worrying about it, I chose to forget about it and remind myself that I am abundant. About a week later, I received an unanticipated check in the mail that more than covered it.

NEVER put your attention and focus on what you do not intend. If you do, you will attract precisely the opposite of what you desire. There aren't vibrational equivalents to "no," "not," or "never" in the Universe. It's as if those words don't exist, and the Universe doesn't hear, feel, or respond to them. I started this paragraph with "never" to grab your attention. ALWAYS put your attention and focus on what you do intend and desire.

For example, if you think/feel/believe:

"I don't want to be broke." The Universe hears/feels:
"I ~~don't~~ want to be broke."
"I don't want to be sick." The Universe hears/feels:
"I ~~don't~~ want to be sick."
"I never want to be alone." The Universe hears/feels:
"I ~~never~~ want to be alone."

Engulf yourself in good feelings appropriately, as much as possible. Feed your mind with positive thoughts, books, movies, conversations, etc.

The highest emotion/feeling is enlightenment, and the lowest is shame. Their corresponding electromagnetic waves, called vibrational pulse points, are measured in Hertz (Hz). One Hz means it's pulsing, or vibrating, once per second. Not surprisingly, the top half of feelings and emotions pulse much faster than the lower half.

Regardless of how you are feeling, the core of your being is love, unconditional love. That is who you really are, who all of us are, at the center of our beings, even though it sometimes doesn't feel like it.

Love is like the sun. It's always there, but we don't see it at night, when it's rainy or cloudy. Like the sun never stops shining, our inner spirit is always unconditionally loving us.

> *If you want to find the secrets of the universe, think in terms of energy, frequency, and vibration.*
>
> ~Nikola Tesla

Section 2

Tips, Tricks, and Tools

Our deepest fear is not that we are inadequate.

Our deepest fear is that we are powerful beyond measure.

It is our light, not our darkness that most frightens us.

*We ask ourselves,
"Who am I to be brilliant, gorgeous, talented and fabulous?"*

Actually, who are you not to be?

You are a child of God.

Your playing small does not serve the world.

There's nothing enlightened about shrinking so that other people won't feel insecure around you.

We are all meant to shine, as children do.

We were born to make manifest the glory of God that is within us.

It's not just in some of us; it's in everyone.

As we let our own light shine, we unconsciously give other people permission to do the same.

As we are liberated from our own fear, our presence automatically liberates others.

~Marianne Williamson

Advocate for Your Success

As you begin this journey, you may observe that many people, perhaps yourself included, can rattle off a long list of everything they do not want or like, or even hate. It's okay to know what these things are because it provides contrast to help guide you towards what you do want, like, and love.

Feel your worthiness with whatever you intend to be, do, or have. This creates vibrational alignment with the actual person, place, thing, or experience you intend to create. It opens up space, allowing you to receive it.

The Power of Imagination

You can literally imagine your future into a reality. And, as you begin to sincerely believe it, this releases resistance and opens you to receiving, which is known as the Law of Allowing.

I love what the great motivational speaker Les Brown said, "Operate out of your imagination, not your memory." This is the secret to acquiring whatever you desire to be, do, or have! It is the sweet spot where you intersect your dreams, goals, and intentions with the feeling of already having them.

Albert Einstein, the famous physicist, said, "Imagination will take you everywhere. Imagination is everything. It is the preview of life's coming attractions."

How do you do this? Simple...be a kid again! Imagine and pretend you already have whatever you intend to be, do, or have. The definition of "pretend" says it all: "Speak and act to make it appear that something is the case when, in fact, it is not."

Abraham/Esther Hicks says: "Never mind what is. Imagine it the way you want it to be so that your vibration is a match to your desire. When your vibration is a match to your desire, all things in your experience will gravitate to meet that match every time." She also reminds us that "worrying is using your imagination to create something you don't want." We all worry. As soon as you catch yourself, gently move away from these thoughts.

For about the first seven years of life, our brain waves are mainly in Theta, which is associated with imagination and a state of hypnosis. It was our magical time. When we were kids imagining, we had no limiting thoughts, doubts, or resistance. We lived in the moment of whatever we were imagining or pretending. Our "pretend" became instantly real.

As adults, visualization is a term we often use. It means the formation of a mental image of something. Either way you prefer to think about it, be a kid again, and imagine, pretend, or visualize your future life.

Another term for the same idea is Mental Rehearsing, a technique often used by athletes. Swimmer Missy Franklin, who won four gold medals at the 2012 London Games, uses visualization to reduce anxiety about the unknown. She said, "When I get there, I've already pictured what's going to happen a million times, so I don't actually have to think about it."

Each technique works the same way: it carves a path in your brain to your goal. Among other benefits, science shows us that positive visualization can decrease stress, reduce anxiety, increase self-confidence, and enhance motivation.

Breathe

Your breath is your bridge to life; you can only live about four minutes without oxygen. Every one of the trillions of cells in your body requires the nourishment of oxygen. While we need to breathe into our diaphragm, in reality, most of us are taking shallow breaths into our chests, depriving ourselves of oxygen. This also creates a feeling of being unsafe and anxious.

When you find yourself getting anxious about anything and your mind starts spiraling, this is my suggestion: pause and take a deep breath into your belly. Then, take a few more. This will calm your nervous system and bring your focus away from your thoughts and into your breath, anchoring you to the present moment.

Sometimes I feel anxious, and occasionally, this happens in the company of other people (like at a party). I used to look for an escape: the bathroom, my car, anywhere to be alone.

Now, I start deep breathing wherever I am. Often, someone will notice and inquire if I am okay. I'll say, "Yes, I am feeling anxious and need to center myself by taking a few deep breaths." Do you know what happens? Everyone around also pauses, and we all take a few deep breaths together. Then everyone smiles and says they feel better.

Check in with yourself three (or more) times a day. Schedule time with yourself to center and breathe. Set a reminder on your phone if that helps. Sit comfortably or lie down, and take six long, deep, slow breaths in from your nose to the base of your belly. Exhale slowly, either through your nose or mouth, for a count of six. This takes about one minute.

This one minute of focused breathing brings oxygen to nourish the cells in your body and brain and also reduces the production of cortisol (a stress hormone). Your brain will tell your nervous system you are safe, and you will feel more relaxed.

I posted a guided video for you on my YouTube channel, Lean Into Your Light.

Shifting to Desire and Intention

As I mentioned earlier, the words we think and speak have a profound influence on shaping our lives. Each of us has the ability to make simple shifts in our verbiage, allowing us to feel better (AKA, alter our energy and vibration). This will enable you to attract the people, experiences, and material objects you desire. Deciding to become more aware of the words you choose is where we begin. While intentional language choice is always important, three words to pay special attention to are: want, desire, and intend.

The word "want" means deficient or shortage. When you want something, it makes you notice it's not there, it's missing from your life, and you believe you need it to feel better. It creates a void, an emptiness, a feeling of lack. I define "want" as actively missing something (or someone) you don't have.

"Want" is a common, everyday word we frequently use. The purpose here is not to eliminate it from your vocabulary. I use it every day, but not when it comes to consciously creating my future. Every day, I say things like, "What do you want for dinner?" or "The dog wants out," or "Do you want to watch a movie?" etc.

There is a totally different energy around saying, "I want Chinese food for dinner," and "I want one million dollars." The Chinese food is an easy fix. Call and order takeout or go to the restaurant. The million dollars statement usually has some resistance around it.

The key point is being aware of how and when you use the word "want." Suppose you focus intently on wanting something you currently lack, like money. In that case, you will start to notice and, more importantly, feel the difference between the money you currently have in your bank account and the amount of money you prefer to have in your bank account. This creates a gap, and you will experience the not-so-good feeling of the absence, or lack, of money. The next two better word options are "desire" and "intend."

Desire is defined as a strong feeling of wanting to have something or wishing for something to happen. It's an improvement over wanting, as it has less resistance. If you doubt your desire, it has a low vibration. However, when you have faith and eagerly anticipate that your desire will happen, it becomes a decision, raising the frequency of your desire. I will use the word "desire" with this understanding.

When my son read a very early draft of this book, he told me that "desire" sounded like a need. I thought about it, and he was right. Desire is a need, which is defined as requiring something because it is essential or very important.

An even better word I am suggesting is "intend." An intention is often understood as an aim or a plan. It is a clearer vision of your future. An intention is a vow to yourself and to the universal will. As mentioned earlier, this is known as Sankalpa, which means to become one with your subconscious mind, connecting with your heart's deepest desire. It is your vow to the Universe, why you are here, and your purpose for being here. It is your contribution to humanity.

From now on, when it comes to sculpting your future, practice shifting your thinking from a list of "wants" to "desires" and "intentions." This is a subtle yet very powerful choice.

We live in a physical body and world, and we all have strong material desires that are necessary for our survival: a healthy body & mind, meaningful relationships, and enough money to live on this planet. Keep it in balance.

Having said that, below is an example of a common material desire, which is a necessity for most of us…transportation. You can replace "car" with anything you might desire. As long as you are going to drive a car, you might as well get one you like!

Say each of these statements out loud and notice the difference in how they feel:

"I want to buy a new car in May."
"I desire to buy a new car in May."
"I intend to buy a new car in May."

The "want" statement feels less definite, like if it doesn't happen, don't sweat it. The "desire" statement feels better; it has more momentum than the "want" statement. The "intend" statement is more solid, weightier, and feels real, as if it will happen!

However, the most powerful words to manifest your desires and intentions are "I AM." The last section of this book is devoted entirely to the power of these two tiny words. Say out loud:

"I AM buying a new car in May."

As you say the words, feel the exciting feeling of having your new vehicle (or whatever it is). In a short period of time, things will fall into place; you will see the right car in the right color at the right price. Don't think too hard about it. Be playful and eager while anticipating its arrival in your life. Trust that it is on its way to you. Whether it happens precisely in May, or sooner, or maybe a few months out, the point is that you are intentionally carving a path to your new vehicle (or whatever it is). It is about the manifestation, not the timeline.

As you are commanding and declaring it to happen, go out and test drive that car! And carry that feeling with you when you drive your current vehicle. Imagine you are driving your new vehicle. Or go shoe or house shopping, whatever it is for you.

It's magical when you hold your intention and pretend you already have whatever it is. Have faith in this process; it works! Faith is believing in something you can't see, feel, touch, or taste. The best definition of faith I have found is "unwavering certainty." I also think of it as an "unshakable knowing" that it will happen, whatever "it" is.

And, as contradictory as this may sound, you have let go of the outcome. This means that you are okay whether or not it shows up. There are many times when NOT getting what you desire is best at the time.

The all-knowing Universe has got your back on this! You may realize in three months or 30 years the reason it was best not to get it. Or you may feel like you never understood why, yet be accepting, have faith, and know it was in your best interest.

Here's an example of letting go: About a year ago, I decided I wanted a different vehicle. I drive a lot for my current job and wasn't feeling good in my SUV, which I purchased thinking it would be good for transporting the dogs. It didn't work out to be that great for the dogs, and it wasn't really a 'me' car. When I decided to look for another vehicle, I got obsessive about it. I started scouring websites and stopping by dealerships. I was looking so hard, not finding what I intended to purchase, and I was getting frustrated. Rather than relaxing, visualizing and trusting the process I know works miracles, I became fixated on getting a new car. After about a month, I gave up the search and let it go.

Then, about nine months later, I took my car in for an oil change. Usually, I take the shuttle they offer and go home while the car is being serviced. But this was a beautiful September day, and I got the nudge to stay the expected 90 minutes and take Mango (one of my dogs) for a stroll. While walking her, I spotted it at the far front end of the lot: the car I had been obsessively looking for and then gave up on! I would have missed it if I had not trusted my nudge and taken the shuttle home. I traded in my SUV that afternoon and drove my new car home.

The Top Three

The top three things people talk and think about manifesting in their lives are:

1. Health
2. Wealth
3. Relationships

Here are three examples to go with the above list:

Health: I am feeling great at my ideal weight of _____ pounds by _____ or sooner.

Most people use the common language of how many pounds they desire to lose. Phrasing it that way keeps you focusing on losing weight and potentially losing the same 15 pounds over and over. Most of the things we lose are items we want to find, like our keys, wallet, or phone. Once you lose weight, do you want to find it again? I think not! Instead, give your attention to feeling great at your ideal weight.

Wealth: Use this language from the late, great, self-help author Bob Proctor: "I am so happy and grateful now that money comes to me in increasing quantities, through multiple sources on a continuous basis." Insert the specific amount you desire. "I am feeling so grateful now that I am receiving $_____ per month," or I am so happy and grateful having $_____ savings in my bank account."

Relationships: This could be romantic, a new friend, or a business partner. "I am feeling happy and grateful now that my new (partner/friend/business associate) has arrived in my life. S/he possesses all the qualities that are important to me in this relationship."

As you read through this book, you will learn how important it is to refine your language. Initially, you might start by copying the examples word for word. Eventually, you will clarify them to reflect your own words.

By the way, please know it's never too late. And, if you think it's too late, or you're too old, or whatever other excuses you come up with, meet Minette. When I was growing up, we had a neighbor, Minette. She was delightful and, I believe, in her late 60's. She said she always wanted to go to continue her education, so with some encouragement from her friendly neighbors, she enrolled in our local college. One of her concerns was that the young students wouldn't like or accept her because of her age. After her first class, she was beaming! The "kids" in her class loved and embraced her being there. They praised her for having the courage to finally fulfill her dream. She is still an inspiration to me, and I hope for you too.

Anna Mary Robertson Moses, aka Grandma Moses, is one of the most prolific artists ever known. She didn't start painting until she was 77 years of age. Hallmark purchased the rights to her paintings, which they, in turn, reproduced on greeting cards, and Grandma Moses became a household name. She exhibited her work internationally until she was in her 90s and continued to paint a total of over 1,500 images until a few months before her death at age 101.

There are many more examples. These are a couple that hold a special place in my heart.

No Regrets

I wish I'd had the courage to live a life true to myself, not the life others expected of me.

~Bronnie Ware

This is the #1 regret according to the book, *The Top Five Regrets of the Dying* by Bronnie Ware, a hospice nurse.

The most common regret people have at the end of their lives isn't what they did but what they didn't do. Sydney J. Harris, an American journalist, said this: "Regret for the things we did can be tempered by time; it is regret for the things we did not do that is inconsolable." Another American Journalist, Norman Cousins, said, "Death is not the greatest loss in life. The greatest loss in life is what dies inside us while we live."

What's inside you that wants to be birthed? We are creative beings here to express our unique gifts. We are all here for a reason. You are not just a visitor to Earth, you are here to do something uniquely yours in this life. Do not let another moment of your precious life pass by without being fully you. As Les Brown says, "Don't take your dreams to the grave."

Go to your journal or poster board and write your own bucket list. Who do you intend to be? What do you intend to do or have in this life that you would regret not experiencing?

Of the billions of people on our planet there is only ONE of you. We are all part of a giant jigsaw puzzle; without YOU, the puzzle is missing a piece and is incomplete. You and all of your beautiful talents and imperfections.

There is a saying that goes something like, "There is a crack in everything. That's how the light gets in."

I believe that through our cracks, we let our light shine out!

> *Your time is limited, so don't waste it living someone else's life.*
>
> ~Steve Jobs

We are not guaranteed tomorrow. So, the best time to live the life you imagine and to fulfill your dreams, goals, and intentions is now. The time is now to become the most authentic version of yourself. So, laugh and smile more. Enjoy the present moment.

"Don't let fear fuel your choices. Live fearlessly. Run toward life. Don't worry about what people will think," said Kerri Grote while dying of brain cancer. She also said, "Surround

Lean Into Your Light

yourself with people who contradict that unkind voice, people who see your light and remind you who you are: an amazing soul." I happened to read this in a Facebook post. Thank you, Kerri, and rest in peace.

The beautiful Deshauna Barber, crowned Miss USA in 2016, who serves in the Army reserves and is a motivational speaker, says: "Do not fear failure, but please be terrified of regret." Look up her inspiring story on YouTube.

Writing this book is an example of no regrets. There was no turning back once I received the inspiration to write it. I *had* to do it. The impulse to write it overrode my fearful thoughts. It flowed from somewhere inside me to my hands to write notes and then onto my keyboard. It felt as if a portal opened deep inside of me. Inspiration and divine guidance helped me research and find the perfect words, quotes, and examples to best communicate these ideas.

I easily found the perfect information I needed at the right time. That's how most of the quotes in this book came to me. It was even delivered to me in a fortune cookie that said, "You create your own stage. The audience is waiting."

Occasionally, I had thoughts of self-doubt. I also knew I would regret it for the rest of my life if I didn't take the chance to write and publish this book. What was I afraid of? Fear of failure? Fear of success? Both?

Then I not-so-randomly came across this quote I hadn't heard before:

Do not be dismayed by the brokenness of the world.
All things break.
And all things can be mended.
Not with time, as they say, but with intention.
So go.
Love intentionally, extravagantly, unconditionally.
The broken world waits in darkness for the light that is you.

~L.R. Knost

Emotions and Feelings

Feeling is the fuel that manifests thoughts into physical form.

~Justin Perry

Did you know there is a difference between emotions and feelings? Until I began researching for this book, I didn't fully understand the distinction between the two. We tend to use these words interchangeably in everyday conversation. While they are both energy, they have different meanings.

We feel strong emotions when we experience an unexpected situation (perceived as good or bad). Our brains then release chemicals into our bodies. Emotions are found on either the high or low end of the vibrational scale, not in the middle. It's your brain's spontaneous reaction to an event, and you cannot control it from happening. An example of this is a few days after the Hamas attack in Israel, I was leading a meditation for my yoga class. As we expanded our loving-kindness meditation across the globe, I suddenly felt a rush of grief and sadness, and tears flooded into my eyes. This experience was unanticipated.

I posted an example of a loving-kindness meditation on my YouTube channel, Lean Into Your Light, for you.

Think about when you have gotten emotional about something. It suddenly welled up inside and had to come out like suddenly bursting into tears or exploding in laughter. This is why we have expressions like, "S/he was overcome with emotion." While you can't control your emotions from happening, you can learn to manage and cultivate what happens next, which are your feelings. Feelings tend to last longer than emotions.

Feelings occur all day up and down the emotional scale; they are less intense than an emotion. Feelings also arise on their own, and you have the power to consciously create them, unlike emotions, which are mostly unconscious and spontaneous, as mentioned above.

An example is you're in a good mood and hear a song that reminds you of a breakup. Then you listen to all the sad songs you know, look at old photos, talk to your friends about it, watch sad movies, etc. You have just created the feeling of sadness. And this is okay if it helps you process and move through residual feelings. The point is that you made this happen.

How do you manage your feelings? First, become aware of and acknowledge your current feeling(s). The higher vibrational feelings are easy: happiness, love, joy, etc. These are empowering and you want to bask in them as long as you can!

Lean Into Your Light

There is a simple recipe to create feelings of happiness: do things that make you happy. To create gratitude, focus on what you are grateful for, and to create joy, do and speak of things that give you joy! Make a list of what makes you happy and refer to it when you need a reminder. I have a list of about 15 things that make me happy. If I'm feeling down or need direction, I read my list. Just reading it makes me feel better. Create your own list of what makes you happy on page 134.

The lower-end feelings may be tricky at first, particularly if you haven't yet learned to befriend and name these uncomfortable feelings. You will get better with practice, or you can ask for help from a trusted friend or family member to help you name your feelings. When you learn to recognize and name these feelings, they won't feel as often awkward as they once did. However, some are disempowering and just plain toxic. You want to process them as quickly as possible, such as shame, rage, jealousy, and envy. And you do need to process them. You cannot just shove them under the rug. If you do that, eventually they will lay there and fester. They will manifest and surface in undesirable ways, including illness, until you do the work by looking at them and understand as best you can, what the lesson is for you. That is when you can truly release them and become a little more enlightened on your self-discovery journey.

It may seem odd to expand upon the low vibration, disempowering feelings in a book about manifesting your dreams and intentions, but it's essential because this is life, and it is going to happen to you.

You will rightfully feel anger at someone or a situation. Usually, it's because someone crossed your boundaries in some way. Anger, used properly, can be a great tool and motivator. As Gandhi said, "Anger can be like electricity: It is just as powerful, but only when we use it intelligently and effectively."

Todd Kashdan and Robert Biswas-Diener's book, *The Upside of your Dark Side: Why Being Your Whole Self -Not Just Your "Good" Self - Drives Success and Fulfillment*, shares how appropriately expressing anger can lead to more successful negotiations and, surprisingly, increase your creativity.

One of the hormones your body releases is adrenaline, which, among other effects, boosts your energy supply. I was upset about a situation last week. Usually, I go outside and walk it off or get on my bike and ride it out. This particular morning, it was too cold for me to go outside, so I took that energy (adrenaline) and cleaned out part of my closet. I had meant to do it anyway, and I used this task to move the energy through me. About an hour later, I felt better and my closet was more organized. Writing about this a week or so later, I don't even remember what I was mad about!

As for loss and sadness, there will be a time in your life when you experience deep grief at the passing of someone you love, whether that be a human or a pet. Waves of grief can sometimes feel as if they've taken over your entire life. At the heart of grief is love, and it's essential to allow yourself to go through and process the grief cycle. Author Jamie Anderson states, "Grief, I've learned, is really just love. It's all the love you want to give but cannot. All that unspent love gathers up in the corners of your eyes, the lump in your throat, and in that hollow part of your chest. Grief is love with no place to go."

If this is the case for you, it may or may not be a good time for you to go into your positive "I AM" statements. Everyone grieves differently. If you find a few that are soothing, use them. If you are feeling resistant, come back later.

Sometimes, when I feel extremely sad, and nothing seems to lift my mood, I listen to the REM tune *Everybody Hurts*. This reminds me I am not alone, and it happens to every one of us on this human journey we call life.

Make sure to acknowledge them when you are feeling tired, frustrated, or angry. Say to yourself, out loud, or to another person, "I am feeling tired," rather than saying, "I am tired." Being tired is a feeling, and it will pass. Being hungry or thirsty is also a feeling. All our feelings come and go. We say, "I am hungry," but actually, your body needs nourishment, and it will pass after you have something to eat. I prefer the way it's said in Spanish, "tengo hambre," "I have hunger," "tengo sed," or "I have thirst," which is more accurate.

For all the feelings on the lower part of the vibrational scale, get into the habit of thinking and saying "I feel" rather than "I am." You don't want to *become* the lower scale of emotions and feelings, especially shame, jealousy, and rage, to name a few.

However, for the higher vibration, empowering feelings, you want to authentically align yourself as one with: "I am joyous," "I am appreciating," or "I am loved." The book's last section is devoted to these empowering "I AM" statements.

Now that you know your words carry vibrations and energy with the passion and conviction they are thought or spoken, be conscious of the feelings, energy, and emotions you put into your "I AM" affirmations. They will deepen their influence on your mind, and you will manifest more quickly. Make sure your emotions and feelings behind your words, spoken and unspoken, are of as high of a vibration, as appropriate, most of the time.

Remember, your emotions and subsequent feelings create vibrational and energetic movement throughout your physical body, out to the world around you, and through the universe.

Many people don't know about the power of good feelings, and so their feelings are reactions or responses to what happens to them. They have put their feelings on automatic pilot, instead of deliberately taking charge of them.

~Rhonda Byrne

Now, close your eyes and imagine your ideas, dreams, and feel your future intentions already in your life! Write them down in your journal or on a poster board (I used both). Writing things down increases your memory retention. It creates and solidifies new neural pathways in your brain and changes your thought patterns. Your brain thrives on patterns!

I created vision boards of my intentions using gold and purple Sharpies. I wrote my "I AM" statements and added pictures of what I intend to do, be, and have.

Writing down your future wishes is a first step. Then, the key is to cultivate and match their vibrational frequency. Your thoughts, emotions, feelings, moods, and attitudes change physical matter on a cellular level. This, in turn, attracts your intentions, desires, and dreams to you. With practice, it gets easier.

Here is the simple, three-step recipe I used to manifest my dream of writing this book:

1. Intention: Publishing this book

2. Expectation: Create the feeling your intention is real, right now, in the present moment: "I am feeling excited my book is serving others."

3. "I AM" statement of my intention: "I am the author of the best-selling book *Lean Into Your Light*."

Now it's your turn:

1. State your intention:

   _____

2. Create your expectation:

   _____

3. "I AM" statement of your intention:

   _____

The Guest House

This being human is a guest house.
Every morning a new arrival.

A joy, a depression, a meanness,
some momentary awareness comes
as an unexpected visitor.

Welcome and entertain them all!
Even if they're a crowd of sorrows,
who violently sweep your house empty of its furniture,
still treat each guest honorably.
He may be clearing you out for some new delight.

The dark thought, the shame, the malice,
meet them at the door laughing,
and invite them in.

Be grateful for whoever comes,
because each has been sent
as a guide from beyond.

~Rumi

Believe

Your subconscious mind accepts the dominant of two ideas.

~Joseph Murphy

The more you hear something or the more it's repeated, internally or externally, the more you begin to believe it. True or not, it becomes a belief. A belief is "an acceptance that a statement is true or that something exists." Beliefs are very powerful. Whether they come from others, the media, or your mind, when continuously repeated, they become core beliefs, again, whether they are true or not.

There was a time when people believed the world was flat, even when they could look in the night sky and see that all the planets and stars were round.

Not that long ago, there was an accepted belief that no one

could run a mile in four minutes (or less). In 1954, at age 25, Roger Bannister broke the four-minute barrier! He shattered this false belief, and now it is the standard. Thousands of people are known to have broken it. In 1983, Cliff Young, a 61-year-old potato farmer, won and set a new world record for one of the most grueling marathons in the world. He ran the Australian ultra-marathon, an annual ultra endurance course without sleeping. Before Cliff, runners believed they needed 18 hours of running daily and about six hours of sleep a night. But Cliff did not know this! He ran it without sleeping. Now, his experience has set a new standard.

What false beliefs are you holding on to? Write them down on page 139. Where they came from is not important at this stage. You can overcome your negative and false beliefs with awareness and thoughtful work.

Just as important as your false, old beliefs is to recognize when you begin to doubt yourself. The moment you notice insecurities, hesitancies, or indecision regarding your future ability to achieve your goals, *immediately* pivot your thoughts in another direction.

For example, as I was writing this book, sometimes I had the thought pop into my head *this is stupid, just give up*. The moment I caught myself, I said to myself and sometimes aloud, "No, no, no, no." That's when I reached for my favorite I AM statements: I am worthy. I am deserving. I am receiving. These pushed the fear and worry away. It helped keep my mind focused on my future.

Lean Into Your Light

When this happens to you, your scary, self-defeating words may be different, however the process is the same. Quickly get away from the mind-chatter before any momentum builds and you start to fall down that negative rabbit hole. Shift to any I am statement in the back of the book that makes you feel good. Shift to anything that makes you feel better.

There are many examples in this world, and in your own life, of people that experienced their own hardships, yet they all have one thing in common: their mindset on their future. No matter what the circumstance, they kept going in the direction of their dreams. They kept their eyes on the prize.

A few very famous people you may not realize had a rough start. They kept their focus on the outcome they sought and eventually achieved:

-Michael Jordan was cut from his high school basketball team.

-Steve Harvey lived in his car for 3 years.

-Dolly Parton was born into extreme poverty.

When you get to the point of integrating an "I AM" statement that you don't yet totally believe, and you really want to cultivate it, continue to confidently repeat it, both internally and out loud daily. Also, write it down. You will probably experience a feeling of discord between your old and new beliefs, which is to be expected and quite normal. The fancy name for this is Cognitive Dissonance, which means: "The mental conflict that occurs when beliefs or assumptions are contradicted by new information." Most likely, it will also feel uncomfortable and often scary. This is normal. It's also a habit, so give it 30 days or so to shift. If you are at odds between an old belief and your new one, give it a break and return to it later.

As you become aware of the false beliefs you have been carrying around, you will begin the pivotal transformation process. It's a permanent, irreversible shift in your beliefs and behaviors. That is how you will achieve your desired results.

Whatever you believe with emotion becomes reality.
You always act in a manner consistent with your innermost beliefs and convictions.

~Brian Tracy

Cultivate a Gratitude Practice

To create an environment for your personal success, write lists of things you are grateful for. Why make a gratitude list? Dr. Joe Dispenza states it clearly, "Gratitude is the ultimate state of receivership."

The best dictionary definition I found is on vocabulary.com, which says, "Gratitude, which rhymes with "attitude," comes from the Latin word gratus, which means "thankful, pleasing." An attitude of gratitude, as the common phrase goes.

To start, use the back of this book, then find a journal you love and/or poster boards. Make lists of what makes you feel a spark, a jolt for your life and makes your heart sing. Make lists of who and what you appreciate and are grateful for. Do this daily. I suggest in the morning and before bed to "bookend" your days. If you feel stuck when you begin, go ahead and make a list of everything you don't like or that makes you unhappy, then pivot each. For example, if you don't want to be sick, spin it to "I am grateful for my health." There is space in the back of this book to get your lists going on page 135.

Another suggestion is to write your lists of gratitude, happiness, and "I AM" statements (more on this soon) using your favorite-colored Sharpies or pens—gold and purple (my first choices) or any colors that appeal to you.

Handwriting and re-reading what you wrote anchors your lists more securely in your conscious and subconscious mind. Make your journal, or this book, your trusted companion. Bring it everywhere.

To consciously get your positive feelings flowing, write a gratitude and appreciation list for everything you do have and use your list as a bridge for your future intentions. Cultivate a daily attitude of gratitude. Tell someone how much you appreciate them. Call, text, or send them a beautiful card expressing your appreciation. The simplest expression of gratitude and appreciation is a heartfelt, "Thank you."

Focusing on gratitude and appreciation releases hormones (dopamine, serotonin, endorphins, and oxytocin) which play a role in feeling pleasure. It also has many other benefits, including improving physical and mental health, relationships, and more.

Dopamine is one of the neurotransmitters that activates the Reticular Activating System (RAS), a bundle of nerves at the bottom of your brain stem. Your RAS creates filters to show you what you think about and focus on. It doesn't differentiate between reality and fantasy/pretending/visualizing. It only knows what you focus on and searches to find more of it. For example, when you cultivate thoughts of gratitude and appreciation, your RAS will find you more things to be grateful for. Or, when you are thinking about getting a new red car. You begin to see red cars everywhere! Simply stated, this is the science that explains the Law of Attraction.

Music

You know what music is? God's little reminder that there's something else besides us in this universe: harmonic connection between all living beings, everywhere, even the stars.

~Robin Williams in August Rush

Music is the most straightforward example of vibration. Listen to music that uplifts you and makes you feel good. It's a quick, easy, and simple way to raise your vibration. Choose songs that put a smile on your face and perhaps bring back good memories. As I write this book, I am listening to music that makes me feel happy.

I am keenly aware of the effect music has on me. Recently, I heard a song on the radio that brought up bad memories for me. Although I like the song by U2, I changed the station and listened to something else that made me feel better.

Become consciously aware of what, where, and who makes you feel peaceful, happy, appreciated, or any other positive internal state. Now, honor these above all else.

You already know that certain music can make you happy, calm, or sad. So, listening to music is an easy way to alter or enhance your mood. Generally, you want to choose something to feel better, but sometimes we all need to listen to a sad song and have a good cry. Processing your "negative" (low vibration) emotions and feelings is healthy.

> *Music is a language that doesn't speak in particular words.*
> *It speaks in emotions, and if it's in the bones, it's in the bones.*
>
> ~Keith Richards

Colors

Our relationship with a certain color says something about our relationship with the part of our consciousness that the color represents.

~Sir Martin Brofman

Colors play a role in the web of connection between all our senses. They consist of light energy, and each has a unique vibration.

Gold, for example, represents a connection to Source (God, Higher Power, etc.) in the service of humankind. The color gold, not surprisingly, also represents wealth, security, and ease. So, it makes sense why some of us are attracted to gold. When I'm writing, gold is my go-to choice. It just feels right.

Purple is another color I often gravitate towards. Purple is associated with wealth (like gold) and royalty. Livescience.com says that "Purple's elite status stems from the rarity and cost of the dye originally used to produce it." It is also the color associated with your highest emotional vibrations: joy, peace, and enlightenment.

My home office, where I do most of my writing, is rich in colors, primarily hues of gold, red, yellow, and purple. There are splashes of blue and green too. I enjoy being here. I feel happy. Surround yourself with and dress in colors that make you feel good.

Color is vibration like music; everything is vibration.

~Marc Chagall

Patience and Repetition

Repetition breeds integration and internalization.

~David Cameron Gikandi

Whatever old beliefs you have took thousands of repetitions to become embedded and programmed in your subconscious. With patience and repetition of the new beliefs you desire and intend, you can change your old thought patterns. Stay consistent. Trust me, it works.

And it's taken me thousands of times of repeating my new desired beliefs that I am worthy, I am deserving, and I am receiving, to truly integrate them into my identity. The truth is, I felt the opposite of this most of my life. When I was younger, some unkind people told me that I was worthless, a loser, and a zero. My subconscious mind recorded this and, for years, did its job by playing it back to me.

Writing and researching this book gave me the tools to change them. Now, I know I am worthy, I am deserving, and I am receiving! When I repeat my mantras, I feel good. I have finally deeply embedded my new beliefs and absolutely know they are true!

The most effective time of day to focus on your desired beliefs is the 20 minutes after you wake up and 20 minutes before falling asleep. These times are considered the gateway to the subconscious; they're very powerful times of your day. This is when your mind is most easily influenced and impressionable. It is when you can most deeply change your subconscious programming…that autopilot tape that plays over and over again.

Focus on your chosen "I AM" statements, appreciations, and expressions of gratitude. It's very important to consistently dedicate yourself to practicing them. You can train yourself in this important habit with perseverance, determination, and practice. Overriding your false subconscious beliefs is a process. Be patient with yourself.

Putting your attention to your chosen mantras in a positive, relaxed, receptive mode will, over time, gradually and naturally become your default mode. Become the master of your thoughts, not an indentured servant to negative, disempowering, repetitive ones. It is estimated that we think between 12,000 to 60,000 thoughts per day. A whopping 80% are negative, and 95% are exactly the same repetitive thoughts as the previous day. Yikes!

Habits

We first make our habits, and then our habits make us.

~John Dryden

A habit is defined as "an automatic pattern of behavior which is acquired through frequent repetition." You probably don't think about brushing your teeth, locking the front door, and other daily small tasks. You have repeated them so many times your hands just do it. They have become patterns embedded in your brain.

The amount of time it takes to form a new habit can be affected by your level of resistance or non-resistance to the new behavior. For more on habits, I highly recommend reading *The Power of Habit* by Charles Duhigg.

Generally, it's accepted that it takes about 30 days to discipline ourselves to form a new habit. In my experience, it then takes about another 30 days for it to become an automatic, non-thinking action.

When I started this journey, it took me about a month to integrate my chosen "I AM" affirmations into my daily thought patterns. While I continued integrating my "I AM" affirmations into my thoughts and spoken and written words, it took me another month or so to notice significant positive shifts and changes in my life. I went from believing and trusting to now having complete faith in knowing my intentions will manifest.

Then, how come it seems so hard? As humans, we are creatures of habit and resist change, even if it's for the better. Habits are ingrained in us, and when we don't have to think about them, it makes it easy to continue doing whatever it is.

Here is a simple example from my life: There was a time when my morning habit was to have a warm Chai Tea and soymilk latte. Even though I had heard that soy isn't good for your body, out of habit, I kept buying it. One night, I "heard" a voice from deep inside me that said if I kept drinking soymilk, I would get breast cancer. I stopped drinking it immediately. In this case, it was effortless. Instead of automatically going to where the soymilk was, I only had to look for the almond milk. Same aisle, different shelf. It was easy!

When I was a kid, my dad smoked cigarettes and didn't want to quit. One day, he went to the dentist, who told him it looked like he had a precancerous spot on his throat. He quit smoking that day. It took him ten more years to stop drinking, but eventually he did! A change in your habits can take one day, one year, or happen in an instant. Each person and every circumstance are different.

Your good habits (like exercising) improve the quality of your life. Bad habits (like smoking) lower the quality of your life. Of all the bad habits I've observed, talking about your problems is the worst. Swap out talking about problems for what triggers delight, pleasure, and exhilaration for you!

Make a list of your good habits and a list of your bad habits. Take a look and give yourself credit for the good ones! As for the not-so-good ones, decide which ones you will change.

Here are a few habits to be aware of that offer opportunities to improve your quality of life:

Catastrophizing

This is a bad habit, but with awareness and some effort, you can change it. It's a fantastic opportunity for each of us to improve the quality of our lives.

When we were less evolved as a species, to protect us from harm, our brains had to remind us of the dangers we experienced and of stories passed on by others to teach us about potential threats. Our brain is designed to keep us alive by reminding us of all the dangers we have encountered or been told about: don't eat those berries, you will get sick, or to get to the hunting grounds, turn at the big red tree and, oh yeah, it's dark out, and you can't see the bear cave around the bend.

The part of your brain that does this is a small, almond-shaped section called the amygdala. Among other functions, it is responsible for your protection, survival and safety. This is where the fight or flight response trigger is activated sending information to the frontal lobes for interpretation. Interestingly enough, it also holds the emotional, social, learning and communication function. It's concerned with basic survival and self-preservation. It is your threat detector, which is a helpful and essential function of the brain. However, you may know some folks who take it to the point of catastrophizing. They (or maybe you do, too) imagine the worst possible outcome of an action or event. I suggest imagining the best possible outcome!

When you really aren't in imminent danger, there are a number of ways you can interrupt your thinking. The first step is to become aware of your spiraling thoughts. Pause your thinking and focus on anything that doesn't cause resistance, or, if possible, find something that puts a smile on your face – a memory that warms your heart, a photo that does the same, or reach for an I AM affirmation. You can also use any question that interrupts this thought pattern. For example, when I start down the catastrophizing rabbit hole, I stop and ask myself, "Now that it worked out, how do I feel?" I also remind myself that everything always works out the best for me.

Your Morning Routine

Your morning routine is the most important habit for you to cultivate. According to psychologist Ron Friedman, the first few hours of your day are your most precious for maximized productivity. He says, "Typically, we have a window of about three hours where we're highly focused. We're able to make some strong contributions in terms of planning, thinking, and speaking well."

As I mentioned earlier, research confirms the brain is most active, impressionable, and creative immediately before and after sleep. Make this your most important time of the day.

Below is my current morning routine. Except for number one, it's not always in this order, and some activities can be combined with others. Also, I highly suggest avoiding looking at your phone or computer for the first hour of your day:

1. After waking up, I give myself time to become more fully alert. Then, I take three deep breaths. Most of the time, the night before, I picked three "I AM" affirmations and wrote them in my journal. I repeat them to myself for a few minutes. Sometimes I read from a previous entry or write a fresh list.

2. Then, I start moving! I have two dogs who are very excited when they know I am up. I feed them and make a cup of tea.

3. Next is the shower…my favorite place to visualize. I have about 10 minutes to visualize/pretend/fantasize about whatever I intend to attract into my day and life.

4. While walking the dogs, I use this time for my "I AM" statements. However, sometimes, I forget about everything and enjoy the beauty of the trees, flowers, or vineyards I live next to. And this is okay too. As long as you are in a state of calm, peacefulness, and receptivity.

Those days

There are those days when it just doesn't happen that smoothly. For whatever reason, there are mornings when I look at the blank pages in my gratitude/appreciation journal, and my mind doesn't think of anything.

So, instead of forcing myself to write anything inauthentic, I read a few from the last week or month and feel better. If that doesn't cut it, I make an exception and go to my YouTube library on my phone and listen to one of my favorite affirmations. Heads up on this suggestion, however. Make sure the meditation you choose doesn't have commercials. Occasionally, there are mornings when nothing seems to work, so I let it go and move on with my day.

Develop your own morning routine. Use my example, parts of it, or create one of your own.

Our character is basically a composite of our habits.
Because they are consistent, often unconscious patterns,
they constantly, daily express our character.

~Stephen Covey

Meditation

What is meditation? It is simply whatever works for you to quiet your mind. Why is that important? Just as your physical body benefits from rest, so does your mind. Meditation offers an opportunity to get out of your analytical (thinking) mind.

Traditionally, you sit tall on a meditation cushion or the floor and focus on your breath to create mental stillness and bring the body, mind, and senses into balance. There are many different definitions of meditation. Two of my favorite descriptions are "meditation is to become oneself" and "meditation is to get to know oneself."

My personal definition is: "Turn down the volume and change the channel." I direct my mind to neutral or positive thoughts and my breath to get out of my habitual thinking patterns.

I have also realized that I carve out time with the *intention* to meditate. For example, I may set aside 20 minutes with the intention of a traditional meditation, and by the time I quiet my thoughts, 19 minutes have gone by! This is normal and okay. Just achieving a few moments of the reduction of thought will bring you a peacefulness, grounding, and presentness that can last all day.

My other favorite forms of meditation are walking in nature, practicing yoga, riding my bike, listening to music, petting my dogs, and cooking. How you get there is not important. Finding what works for you and doing it is. This is part of "the getting to know oneself" or Svadhyaya, as mentioned earlier.

Sometimes, your meditation will produce spontaneous and unexpected inspirational, positive thoughts and ideas. Welcome them and write them down! I've learned that I won't remember it later. And when you get into a good-feeling state, marinate in it for as long as possible.

I posted this simple one on my YouTube channel, Lean Into Your Light:

1. Start by setting a timer for five minutes. You can increase the time as you practice more.
2. Sit tall or lie down on the floor; use a yoga mat or something to keep you comfortable.
3. Close your eyes and relax your neck, tongue, and jaw.
4. Bring your attention to your breath.
5. Breathe in through your nose into the base of your belly for a count of six, then exhale through your nose for six

counts. Repeat six times. This will be about one minute; repeat a few more times. Or, go as long as you feel inspired.

6. Your mind will wander! Do not attach yourself to any thoughts that arise; let them drift on by like clouds in the sky.

7. Repeat daily.

To know yourself is to be confident.
To be confident is to fearlessly express your potential.

-Andy Puddicombe

Some additional benefits I have noticed from my own meditation practice is I have become more intuitive and confident. By now you know I like to clarify what words mean: Intuition is defined as the ability to know something without any direct evidence or reasoning process. And confidence is developing an intense trust in yourself and the quiet inner knowledge of your capabilities. You can see why developing a consistent meditation practice is so important.

Passwords

Love is the password to every soul.

~Anthony D. Williams

A password is defined as "a secret word or phrase that must be used to gain admission to something."

As you are well aware, in our world of online everything, we need passwords to access all our accounts. The great thing is you have complete control over all your password choices. Since you get to create them, use some combination of positive "I AM" statements for all your passwords.

How many times a day do you log into accounts and enter your password? It's a crazy, daily necessity that I don't enjoy, but I turned it into something useful by creating positive ones.

Use this daily repetition to repeat and reinforce whichever "I AM" statements you want to ingrain in your brain! For example, one of my favorites is "I AM lucky." It makes typing my password fun, and it makes me feel good to be lucky!

One afternoon, I overheard a man telling someone how much he hates entering passwords; I get it. He went on to say all his passwords are some version of "I hate passwords." He is reinforcing something he hates all day long without knowing it. Please don't do this.

> *Say YES to the seedlings, and a giant forest cleaves to the sky.*
> *Say YES to the universe, and the planets become your neighbors.*
> *Say YES to dreams of love and freedom. It is the password to utopia.*
>
> ~Brooks Atkinson

Fitness and Food

Exercise is king. Nutrition is queen. Put them together, and you've got a kingdom.

~Jack LaLanne

Any kind of physical movement boosts your mood and reduces anxiety and depression. Find an exercise you like, such as hiking, running, swimming, cycling, dancing, or yoga. At the very least, walk. The great thing about simply walking is that you only need a good pair of shoes and can do it anywhere! Better yet, skip the shoes and walk barefoot in the sand if you are near a beach.

You can simply and quickly boost your mood by raising your arms over your head, especially the "V" for victory, and looking up. If I have enough space, I like to do the arm movements of the breaststroke. Such activities also increase your energy level and immunity and stimulate the lymphatic system, which helps detoxify your body, reduce tension, increase confidence, and provide many more healthy benefits.

To quickly raise your vibration, here are some examples of the easiest ways to get there:

- Smile/Laugh/Sing
- Move/Exercise/Dance
- Meditate/Deep Breathing/Chanting

All of these suggestions move energy through your body. Smiling (even a fake one to start), laughing, and singing all release hormones such as endorphins and dopamine that tell your brain, "I feel good!"

Let's say you have gotten out of shape and gained some weight. Jumping right into "I am fit," might create some resistance. Start with more general statements such as "I am motivated," "I am alive," or "I am breathing." These are all true.

Eventually, as you begin to become more aware of improving your health and making changes, you will be more in alignment with "I am healthy," "I am strong," or "I am balanced."

Food vibrates too! Feed your body fresh and natural foods, for they, too, not surprisingly, have particular energetic frequencies. Not only do processed foods offer little (if any) nutritional value, but they also have a very low vibration. This is one reason you don't feel so good after eating processed foods. Most food items from a box, package, can, bag, fast food restaurants, etc., are processed foods.

The food you eat has a significant impact on how you feel and how well you think. Your food determines your mood. I know

Lean Into Your Light

that when I don't eat well, I tend to feel sluggish, unmotivated, and a bit depressed. If this is new to you, see page 136 for your own food journal. Log everything you put in your mouth and how you feel five to 20 minutes after eating for one week, including how much water you drink. This is only for you, so be honest! For any foods that don't make you feel good, I recommend to eliminate or reduce them from your diet.

One fundamental reason why what you eat and staying hydrated is so vital to your health is that your gut bacteria manufacture about 90% of the body's serotonin, not your brain.

Speaking of your beautiful brain, it only makes up about 2% of your body weight. Yet, your brain uses:

- About 20% to 30% of your daily energy
- 20% of the air you breathe
- 25% of your total blood flow
- 30% of your water intake
- And a whopping 40% of your nutrients!

Nutrition is beyond the scope of this book, but you can see how vitally important a healthy diet is for your brain and moods. Eating well and exercising are good habits you can quickly cultivate. Getting enough sleep is imperative too.

Make fitness a habit. Motivation is what gets you started.
Habit is what keeps you going.

~Jim Ryun

Releasing Resistance

She was resisting the free flow of the life principle which flows as harmony, beauty, joy, and love.

~Joseph Murphy

Releasing resistance, otherwise known as "letting go," requires you to become aware of what resistance you are holding onto. You might even feel more resistance once you become aware of them. Then, the letting go process can begin! It is also called the Law of Allowing.

It starts with awareness and acceptance. As you release resistance, you make space for allowing and receiving. And as you learn to accept situations as they are (or were, since you can't change the past), you release resistance.

Here is the two-step process:

1. Write your resistances in your journal or on poster boards, not to focus on them, but to get them out of your head. Then, take a look at your list. Your list is a series of words, old thought patterns, and beliefs. Once they are on paper, it's as if writing them down, exposing them out in the open, frees your mind from them. They begin to lose their power. Go to page 139 to get started.

2. Accept them as they are/were. This helps to release the burden and resistance of carrying them around in your head.

When I looked at the list I made, I wondered why I was holding onto a negative comment someone said to me when I was 12 years old. And why was I feeling moments of resistance about publishing this book? I thought people might criticize it. It took some time, but I have mostly let that go now. When the resistance, doubt, and fear thoughts pop up, I have trained myself to quickly recognize them and let them go before they gain momentum. I turn my attention to good-feeling "I AM" statements.

Resistance is a form of fear, and we all feel it. I highly recommend reading Susan Jeffers book, *Feel the Fear and Do it Anyway*.

Make Peace with Your Past

An essential element to feeling better and improving your energy and vibration is to make peace with your past regrets. The past is over and done with. You cannot change it. No matter how often you ruminate over a past situation, you cannot go back and alter it. All the "would haves," "could haves," or "should haves" you can think of will not change the past. We all have done or said something that we now regret, are ashamed of, and wish we could delete from our past. Embrace the lesson you have learned and go forward. You did your best with what you knew at the time. Once you truly learn to accept this, you will free yourself from the shackles, anguish, and remorse of the past. You learned something, so let it go and move on. If you need to make amends with someone or forgive yourself, do it and then put it behind you.

It's painful staying stuck in the past. The story you've been telling yourself about the incident is what is causing your pain. It is embedded in your subconscious. It creates you as a victim, whether you were or not. Whatever it was, it probably happened a long time ago, yet it continues to negatively affect you in the present. And every time you think or speak of it, you bring up negative emotions. When that happens, remember what the Greek philosopher Epictetus said: "It's not what happens to you, but how you react to it that matters."

Your past makes you who you are today: all the good, the bad, and the ugly are threads woven together into your life's tapestry. When I look back on my life, I know there are many more positive, good, and happy threads than sad, negative, and painful experiences. It's what you choose to put your attention on that makes them powerful or not.

There was a time in my life when I focused on, talked about, and relived very painful moments. I now choose to accept and release the past. I feel much better looking forward to my future with childlike wonder, eagerness, and anticipation!

Having said that, I have sought professional therapy a few times which helped me work through some difficult circumstances. It was helpful to get another perspective from a trained expert. If you feel drawn to seek out a skilled specialist, I suggest following your instinct.

Now, my North Star is feeling peaceful, content, and thrilled achieving my intentions, which include writing and publishing this book! Sometimes, old, familiar feelings show up that I am aware of and quickly recognize. I don't entertain or relive them. They are not invited or welcome. I don't give them power over

Lean Into Your Light

me anymore, so I focus on something more pleasing and consciously move forward. For too long, I allowed my past to control me. Not anymore. Doing this has made me feel more confident. Now that I understand that I am in control of what I think and what I allow into my consciousness, my self-esteem has improved immensely.

"Marry your future; court your present; divorce your past," says the philosopher Matshona Dhliwayo. And I say, use your past to refine you, not define you. While you are at it, make peace with your present situation too, even if you are dissatisfied with it. Your power is in the present moment. Your attention and energy are best invested in your future. Go to page 142 to get going on "How My Life Will Look One Year from Now."

Do you want to continue to be a prisoner of your past or a warrior for your future?

Just like driving a car, you have to keep your vision in front of you to move forward. Once in a while, you glance to see what's behind you and put it in neutral or reverse, but you look ahead 99% of the time.

It's the repetition of affirmations that leads to belief. And once that belief becomes a deep conviction, things begin to happen.

~Muhammad Ali

Do Something!

The path to success is to take massive, determined action.

~Tony Robbins

While most of your work is creating clear intentions and vibrational alignment, there are physical actions that must take place. You must also do something to move toward your goals and intentions!

What Tony means by massive and determined is first aligning your mindset: your thoughts, mood, and attitude with your intentions. Then, you are prepared to do something to move you toward your future plans. Check out one of his YouTube videos. You can feel his motivation to coach people to success. He is an excellent example of a person living in authentic harmony with his purpose.

I was inspired to write this book, but it didn't write itself. I had to take the ideas that kept coming to me, research and organize my notes, and type them into my laptop.

There is a saying, "Many a false step is made standing still." It means not taking any action, staying stuck, and failing to take a step forward is a big mistake. Start with baby steps. Pick one thing to do and begin. It creates momentum. Many people get tripped up in analysis paralysis. It doesn't matter where you begin. Just start; do something!

Perhaps you need to:

- Make some phone calls
- Do some research
- Read a book
- Take a class
- Attend a seminar
- Update your resume

Get your "Do Something" list started on page 140.

Inaction breeds doubt and fear. Action breeds confidence and courage. If you want to conquer fear, do not sit home and think about it. Go out and get busy!

~Dale Carnegie

Here are some examples to start taking action toward your intentions:

- For a change in your work/career, it's as simple as updating your resume and getting on job boards. Let your friends and associates know you are open to an opportunity suited for you. This is leveraging your contacts and opening yourself to possibilities.
- Maybe you intend to improve your physical body. Make necessary changes to your eating habits. Get to the gym, yoga studio, or just outside for a walk, whatever appeals to you. Schedule your exercise time on your calendar, like you would for a doctor's or dentist's appointment. This is an appointment with yourself for self-care; no one else can do this for you. Make it the important, consistent, habitual priority that it is.
- If one of your intentions is to nurture your meaningful relationships, carve out date nights with your partner, children, and friends! Make this another essential habit. If distance is an issue, pick up your phone and call (don't text) those you love who live across the country or the globe.
- Most importantly, schedule time for yourself in quiet reflection. Whether it's a formal church setting, out in nature, or any other place that brings you peacefulness, take a retreat from your daily responsibilities. Do this. Often.
- Looking to start a business? Find someone who resonates with you and whom you admire online or in your life who started a successful business. Ask them how they did it. They will be flattered and likely excited to share their story with you because it's hardwired in us to reciprocate, more on this in a moment. Learn all you can from them.

- Make a not-to-do list too. What are time wasters for you? Surfing the web, scrolling too much on social media? One time suck for me was playing Solitaire. Finally, I deleted the app from my phone. Make your Not-To-Do list on page 141.

Reciprocity

Abundance is a dance with reciprocity-what we can give, what we can share, and what we receive in the process.

~Terry Tempest Williams

Why am I devoting pages of this book to the concept of reciprocity? The core of this principle is appreciation, gratitude, and thankfulness.

What you are feeling and saying in your gesture of reciprocity is I am appreciating, I am grateful, and I am thankful. You might not say these exact words, but that is the vibration you emit. The Law of Attraction, which states like attracts like, is activated and works its magic.

Wanting to give back is hardwired into our survival. It takes a village! You are not alone in your journey, and many people are ready, willing, and able to help you. Why? Because it's ingrained in the human species.

By giving and taking, we ensure that other people receive help when they need it, and we receive assistance when needed. Recall how great you feel when you help others? Let others feel that joy as well by allowing them to help you.

The background of the word reciprocity can be traced to the Latin "reciprocus" which means, not surprisingly, "moving back and forth."

According to cultural anthropologists Lionel Tiger and Robin Fox, this is called a "web of indebtedness." It is a "unique adaptive mechanism of human beings allowing for the division of labor, the exchange of diverse forms of goods, the exchange of different services, and the creation of a cluster of interdependencies that bind individuals into highly efficient units." It's a social bond that holds us together. I learned about this in Robert Cialdini's book *Influence: The Psychology of Persuasion*. He refers to reciprocity as a universal tendency in human beings.

For example, you bring something when someone invites you to their home. You don't show up empty-handed. It's taught as a polite gesture, which it is, but the deeper root is reciprocity. Someone gives you a gift, invites you to a party, or helps you somehow; you want to repay or reciprocate the gesture.

Periodically, we'll see a fun trend in paying it forward, where you pay for the coffee for the person behind you or something similar. When this happens, people are generally so surprised, thankful, and appreciative that they will often pay for the person behind them. This is reciprocity. When somebody does something for you or gives you something, it sparks a desire within you to return the favor.

We do some form of reciprocity every day. Think about some examples of reciprocity in your own life. As John Haidt states, "Reciprocity is a deep instinct; it is the basic currency of human life."

To me, it has come to mean it's a form of cooperation, an interconnected, unconditional love for humanity.

Section 3

Golden Words

The "I Am" Process

Success is a process, not an event.

~Gary Halbert

"I AM." These two tiny words are the most powerful in the entire Universe. In any language, the moment you think, feel, or say "I AM," you start creating and manifesting immediately. And you are either creating with high-vibration (empowering) positive thoughts or low-vibration (disempowering) negative ones.

"I AM" is a command and a declaration. The Universe and your subconscious mind hear everything you think, say, and feel strongly about. There is always only one answer after "I AM," which is YES! A resounding YES!

"I AM" opens an invitation and creates a magnetism to draw your desires to you. This is the Law of Attraction, one of the powerful universal laws mentioned earlier. As a reminder, the word attraction means magnetism, so we can also call it the Law of Magnetism.

Once you have thought, it has a vibrational signal, and the neurons in your brain begin to vibrate at that frequency (Law of Vibration). Then those vibrations attract vibrations that match it to you (The Law of Attraction). It is really that simple. You are paving the path to your future through your thoughts, words, and feelings behind them.

One of the purposes of your "I AM" statements is to get centered in the present moment and to feel good NOW.

Write in your journal and/or on your poster boards or on page 142 what your life will look like when all the things you want to accomplish in your life manifest. What is most important is to feel as if you already have them.

Think of the words "I AM" as your magic wand. Use these two tiny golden words to create anything you want to be, do, or have. Your words are so powerful, each one carries its own unique, vibrational, creative signature. Now that you are aware, choose them wisely.

Anytime you start a sentence with I AM,
you are creating what you are and what you want to be.

~Dr. Wayne Dyer

Lean Into Your Light

As you go through this part of the book, if you're not feeling in alignment with a particular "I AM" statement, don't force it. Just move on to another that feels better at the moment. If you attempt to force anything that doesn't feel good, you will create resistance, the opposite of creating good feelings and harmony within yourself.

For example, I started saying to myself, "I am the author of the best-selling book *Lean Into Your Light*. I have been repeating this to myself, saying it out loud and in front of a mirror whenever possible. At first, I felt a little awkward saying it. The more I repeated this, the more I believed it. Now, it feels entirely natural, and it just rolls off my tongue. I feel like I bulldozed a road and cleared away all the debris and obstacles in my mind. It created a freeway to my intention. It's also okay if it's not a best seller. Most important is I completed my purpose, to write and publish this book. If only one person truly benefits from reading it, the ripple effect will live on.

This is a simple three-step process, moving from creating your "I AM" statements to affirmations and, finally, to repetitions to reinforce your I AM statements.

1. The first step is to prepare and declare your "I AM" statements or use the ones I prepared later in this section. Once you create your list, you affirm it and repeat it often. A statement is defined as "a definite or clear expression of something in speech or writing."

2. Continuously affirm your statements.

3. As you repeat your "I AM" affirmations, they will quiet your mind and help you focus on the peaceful place within. The peaceful place within is often called your Inner Being, Soul, Spirit, Source, or God.

As you go through the "I AM" sections, start with three that feel best to you as you integrate them. There are two reasons I suggest the number three. First, it is a divine number and is associated with the Trinity. It means you receive protection, guidance, and help from universal forces. It also refers to the birth-life-death cycle, the mind-body-soul connection, and more. Any multiple of three is very powerful. Second, it's a manageable number.

For your chosen "I AM" affirmations, think, say, and/or write your repetitions three times, or any multiple of three, the most powerful being 3, 6, and 9. It's even more powerful to repeat your affirmations while looking at yourself in a mirror.

Make this book your own. There is, by design, lots of extra space for you to make notes and write your own "I AM" declarations. White out or cross out any that don't feel good to you. If you think it belongs in a different category, move it! As you make your notes, use any colors that appeal to you.

As I mentioned earlier, I wrote my "I AM" statements on poster boards and hung them on my bedroom wall. They were the last thing I saw before I went to sleep and the first thing I saw when I woke up.

When I chose the upcoming "I AM" statements, I used three

criteria:

1. Each affirmation is precisely three words, starting with "I AM."

2. The creating words are in the present tense, the Now, the only time that exists in your subconscious and the Universe.

3. The creating word is also a high-vibration, positive word.

Remember, your "I AM" affirmations can be longer than the three-word criteria I used for this book, which I wanted to keep super simple.

Here are three longer ones that I use often:

"I AM enjoying caring for this precious body I have been given."
"I AM vibrating with the frequency of abundance."
"I AM at peace with my past."

You can also easily integrate this verbally as you interact with others. Consider how powerful your answer will be the next time someone asks, "How are you?"

"I AM _____!"

Integrating this process into your daily life will do more than change you; it will transform you. Change is defined as a response to external influences, where modifying day-to-day action achieves desired results. Whereas transformation is defined as modifying core beliefs and long-term behaviors—often in profound ways—to achieve the desired results. The key word is profound.

Repeat, Repeat, Repeat

Repeat them to yourself often throughout the day, especially when you catch yourself thinking Automatic Negative Thoughts (ANTs), ruminating on the past, or going into a place of doubt. This has been a life changer for me. Now that I keep tabs on my thoughts, when I do start to go into the downward spiral of ANTs, ruminating or starting to doubt myself, I catch myself very quickly. Within a couple of minutes, I turn it around.

When I started this journey, I triggered new thoughts through a text thread of "I AM" statements I kept on my phone. I also wrote some of my favorites on an index card I kept in my wallet. Now, after about six years, they are so ingrained that I can quickly tune into my "I AM" statements in my mind at any moment.

As a reminder, whatever you repeat with focus, attention, and emotion will be drawn to you by the powerful Laws of Attraction and Vibration. Your magnetic body is attracting and drawing experiences into your life by the frequency you are emitting. Become acutely aware of what you are focusing on.

Integration of all you are learning in this book is the key to lasting improvement. Make it part of your daily lifestyle, like breathing and eating, for successful change. If I can do it, you can too!

Lean Into Your Light

Integration is nothing but your complete connection with your spirit.

~Nirmala Srivastava

Relax and trust it will work. If you read this book once and put it on a shelf, you will likely not create any significant or profound changes in your life. Put on your calendar NOW the next date you will re-read, or at least review, this book. I suggest, in the beginning, every 30 days. Remember, we learn by repetition. It will keep you on track.

I'll end this part of the book with the beautiful Sanskrit word Namaste, which is how I end all my yoga classes. My favorite translation is:

I honor the place in you in which the entire Universe dwells.

I honor the place in you which is of love, of truth, of light and of peace.

When you are in that place in you, and I am in that place in me, we are one.

~Namaste~

Visit the Lean Into Your Light website at www.leanintoyourlightbook.com to stay connected with me and other like-minded souls.

Quality of Life

I am just having fun being happy!

A 6-year-old boy says to no one in particular

I am grateful

I am appreciating

I am imagining

I am dreaming

I am envisioning

I am happy

I am satisfied

I am content

I am fulfilled

I am pleased

I am believing

I am trusting

I am faithful

I am kind

I am valuable

I am generous

I am optimistic

I am reliable

I am learning

I am wondering

I am aware

I am blissful

I am free

I am allowing

I am vibrant

I am vibrating

I am creating

I am creative

I am releasing

Lean Into Your Light

I am patient

I am easeful

I am wise

I am blessed

I am blessing

I am harmonious

I am abundant

I am confident

I am courageous

I am talented

I am brilliant

I am positive

I am gifted

I am playful

I am open-minded

I am intelligent

I am articulate

I am expressing

I am dynamic

I am eager

I am ecstatic

I am smiling

I am laughing

I am joyous

I am enthusiastic

I am authentic

I am genuine

I am innovative

I am capable

I am wondrous

I am surrendering

I am accepting

I am savoring

I am becoming

I am changing

I am delighting

I am exquisite

I am magnificent

I am astonishing

I am peaceful

I am brave

I am powerful

I am progressing

I am living

I am grounded

I am mindful

I am flourishing

Your Physical Body

Health is the first wealth.

~Virgil

I am alive

I am healthy

I am strong

I am fit

I am energetic

I am graceful

I am flexible

I am balanced

I am breathing

I am attractive

I am beautiful

I am calm

I am peaceful

I am resting

I am healing

I am healed

Relationships: Family, Friends, Romantic

The greatest thing you'll ever learn is to love and be loved in return.

~"Nature Boy," written by Eden Ahbez

I am loving

I am loveable

I am loved

I am trusting

I am trustworthy

I am treasured

I am forgiven

I am forgiving

I am safe

I am listening

I am heard

I am respectful

I am respected

I am helping

I am helped

I am adoring

I am adored

I am appreciating

I am appreciated

I am complimenting

I am complemented

I am loyal

I am reliable

I am soothing

I am patient

I am cherished

I am valued

I am valuing

I am compassionate

Financial

I am so happy and grateful now that money comes to me in increasing quantities, through multiple sources on a continuous basis.

~Bob Proctor

I am abundant

I am prosperous

I am wealthy

I am worthy

I am deserving

I am receiving

I am successful

I am lucky

I am ready

I am confident

I am rewarded

Spiritual

Just as a candle cannot burn without fire, [wo]men cannot live without a spiritual life.

~Buddha

I am miraculous

I am evolving

I am becoming

I am experiencing

I am awakening

I am softening

I am serving

I am unfolding

I am discovering

I am benevolent

I am observing

I am empowered

I am anchored

I am exploring

I am expanding

I am aligning

I am supported

I am connected

I am protected

I am serenity

I am tranquil

I am tranquility

I am equanimity

I am precious

I am sacred

I am peace

I am joy

I am whole

I am infinite

I am unlimited

I am source

I am divine

I am eternal

My Happy List

My Gratitude List

My Food Journal

Day 1

Breakfast: _____

Lunch: _____

Dinner: _____

Snacks: _____

How I felt

_____

_____

_____

_____

Day 2

Breakfast: _____

Lunch: _____

Dinner: _____

Snacks: _____

How I felt

_____

_____

_____

_____

Day 3

Breakfast: _____

Lunch: _____

Dinner: _____

Snacks: _____

How I felt

_____

_____

_____

_____

Day 4   How I felt

Breakfast: _____   _____

Lunch: _____   _____

Dinner: _____   _____

Snacks: _____   _____

Day 5   How I felt

Breakfast: _____   _____

Lunch: _____   _____

Dinner: _____   _____

Snacks: _____   _____

Day 6   How I felt

Breakfast: _____   _____

Lunch: _____   _____

Dinner: _____   _____

Snacks: _____   _____

Day 7   How I felt

Breakfast: _____   _____

Lunch: _____   _____

Dinner: _____   _____

Snacks: _____   _____

Old Beliefs and Resistances

I Am Releasing

Do Something

Not-To-Do List

How My Life Will Look One Year From Now

About the Author

MaryEllen moved from New York to Northern California to attend San Francisco State University. She received a Bachelor of Science degree in Business Administration/Marketing and enjoyed many years in sales.

As an entrepreneur, she has started several businesses and most recently co-founded a non-profit, Recovery Transportation Systems, and serves on the Board of Directors.

She's also a dedicated fitness enthusiast, having discovered yoga after the birth of her daughter. It became a huge passion, and she enrolled in an Advanced Studies/Teacher Training program with Anne O'Brien. She is an Experienced Registered Yoga Teacher (E-RYT) with the Yoga Alliance and has been leading classes, workshops, and retreats for over 20 years.

When not on her yoga mat, she loves traveling to explore new cultures. Closer to home, she can be found hiking the local hills, walking her dogs, and spending time with family.

www.ingramcontent.com/pod-product-compliance
Lightning Source LLC
LaVergne TN
LVHW011422080426
835512LV00005B/204